What Yellow sounds like

poems by
Linda Susan Jackson

TIA CHUCHA PRESS
LOS ANGELES

ISBN 978-1-882688-33-3

Book Design: Jane Brunette
Cover Illustration: Krista Franklin. Image of Etta James from *Rage to Survive: The Etta James Story,* by Etta James and David Ritz, Da Capo Press, 1998.

PUBLISHED BY: DISTRIBUTED BY:
Tia Chucha Press   Northwestern University Press
A Project of Tia Chucha's Centro Cultural   Chicago Distribution Center
PO Box 328   11030 South Langley Avenue
San Fernando, CA 91341   Chicago, IL 60628
www.tiachucha.com

Tia Chucha Press is supported by the National Endowment for the Arts and operating funds from Tia Chucha's Centro Cultural. Tia Chucha's Café & Centro Cultural have received support from the Los Angeles Department of Cultural Affairs, Los Angeles Community Redevelopment Agency, Trill Hill Foundation, the Center for Cultural Innovation, the Middleton Foundation, Not Just Us Foundation, the Liberty Hill Foundation, Youth Can Service, Toyota Sales, Solidago Foundation, and other grants and donors including Bruce Springsteen, John Densmore, Dan Attias, Dave Marsh, , Denise Chávez and John Randall of the Border Book Festival, Luis & Trini Rodríguez, and others.

Table of Contents

For my husband, Rodney, Sr.
whose love and support
have never wavered

and

my son, Rodney, Jr.
who helped me grow up
all over again

Prologue

I'm four hours old,
wrapped mummy tight.
Through blinding light
she looks at me.
Behind her look
lurks the question
he'll repeat
from 22 months ago
when my brother was born.

He enters the room,
looks from me to her,
spins his hat by the brim,
remembers the doctor
looked past him
to announce my birth.

If he'll just wait a few years,
I'll brown like him,
but he can't see
beyond my blue eyes,
beyond my blonde hair.

My mother turns toward the window,
the question swells in his mouth.

What
Yellow
sounds like

1

sounds like

Dear Miss Etta James,

The youngest and brownest
of my mother's sisters
brought your first album
to grandmother's house,
into her front parlor thick
with claw-footed furniture,
gilded mirrors, oval frames
with faded sepia-toned pictures
and a calendar from *Lane Funeral Parlor*
hanging on burgundy walls
that felt like crushed velvet.

With one note, grandmother said
I didn't come all the way to New York
to hear that gal hoop and holler
behind some man.

At twelve,
even when supervised,
you were taboo. I learned
about waiting until
I was alone.
About sneaking into
my aunt's hiding places.
About ritualizing scarlet
lipstick. Pepsi on ice. Bare
feet. Crossed legs. Eyes
closed. Head back.

Between cackle and crack
as the needle scratched,
your scream and moan
rose from the wax, seized
me with feelings, no words.

Just a sudden urge
to be who I heard

because you know the bark
of the body each time you
twirl that microphone, swing
it between your legs.
That howl is heat.
That purr is pleasure.
That cry is comfort.
That grunt
means *gone*.

Still, the audacity of your baby-blonde hair,
your pear shape, your desperate grace.   Well!

P.S. I wanted to write sooner.

A History of Beauty

Mother told me I'm from a line
of technicolor women with mountains

of breasts and wide laps that held nursing children
or steel bowls filled with June peas. With words,

they were acrobats. Tongues colliding
with a firmness as flexible and specific

as Ma Rainey lyrics, matching memories of bent backs,
third grade geography books, midnight riders,

unplanned births, but there is something more.
Like nightingales, their sounds of love and loss

echo in kitchens, bouncing off hot-plate-brewed
coffee and two-day-old biscuits sopping up Karo

syrup. In their songs they remember the feeling
of that first kiss as they followed their men

to northern cities; men who bit their tongues,
ate dirt, dust and their pride. Worked anywhere.

These women knew only a blues could mask
the painful smell of faces stuck to the goggles

their men wore in steel factories. Now, they have
no time for beauty, theirs left in wind whispering

through bulrush, the teeming taste of scuppernong
grapes, the anticipation of a ham dotted with a patchwork

of cloves spinning on a spit and hints of honey
suckle buried freely in the folds of their flesh.

Beauty's Season

That April when Beauty's daughter was born,
Beauty didn't know she was angry. Twenty years
old, two years married, now with two children.
She didn't call out; her gasp had no precedent,
her words lost in loss with answers that solve
nothing. No time for reflection, so she covered
every mirror. Her vanity drowned under a land
slide of diapers, sterilized bottles, potty chairs
and pacifiers. A working mother because
she had no choice, she became a master
of love at a distance. No need to tie down
the tongue-tied: her thoughts a tempest of tales,
tangled like gossip, growing into a fullness
that remembers the feeling of every first thing
and the velvet violence of a spoiled spring.

Hair

for Cynthia

The story begins as it has from the beginning.
My mother is thankful that there is hair.

Not good. Not bad. Not yet.
I learn what I need to know about

hair, sitting on the floor between
swollen knees. Curiosity moves

my aching head around.
Brush cracks scalp.

I sit stone still.

Your hair's nappy as a sheep's behind,
she says, sucking her teeth, combing

her past and her present in my hair.
On days she hums Sarah Vaughan,

I get two braids. With Etta James,
I'm on the hardwood for hours.

On alternate Fridays, Glover's Mange
washes through my forest of hair.

Scalp stings for two days. On Sundays,
I sit in a high back chair in the kitchen.

Head bent. Chin in chest. Metal comb
lies in flames. I smell last week's sacrifice

on the altar of Madame CJ Walker. Hot comb
slides in slippery hands as it cleans tightly curled

kitchens. My jaws clench; saliva rises in my mouth
with the smell of wet greased protein, burning. Hot

comb teeth marks frame my face with a new
hairline. Smoke trails up from the curling iron

as it cools on a tattered towel. I hold my ear
for Shirley Temple curls. What I get are bent

ends that curve Royal Crown stiff. No bounce.
No dance. No bojangle. At night, hair set

in brown paper, wire, plastic or sponge tied up
in a stained scarf, I dream of a time before my hair

was straightened, nearly dead, when rain,
a swim or a sweat didn't frighten my roots.

How Much for
the Little Girl

On a dock, the day still with
anticipation, Agamemnon's
appetite draws the press
of his pride. His speech
reeks of deceit as he entreats
his daughter, *Come, my lamb.*
Walk with me (the distance
between a smile and a lie).

Iphigenia peers into her father's
eyes. Tears flood their cheeks
as she seeks an answer to the
question of her worth. The only
sound now is the sudden breeze
as it slaps and whips waves on all
sides of the ships, for she knows
she is the price of a favorable wind.

Etymology

Again she points to the primer,
and my brother skips that first

word – *it*. Again our mother
slaps him, and my face stings

as his puffs up blood-red. My
eyes plead with him — read, just

read the word. He does not cry
or comply. My legs sweat under

a coffin-stiff cotton dress
hooped out by a crinoline

that scratches like sandpaper,
the vinyl seat sticking to my legs.

My brother, his plaid shirt tucked
neatly in his dungarees, is all I have.

We share every thing: a room, toys,
secrets, the strap when she says

Get to the back and take off your clothes.

Two years apart, we have spent
over fourteen hundred days

as brother and sister, so close
they call us grandpa and grandma.

That last slap left the air so thick
we still taste the threat living here,

so I invent a word game — starting
with *ma* — to imagine our mother

as the smallest element of meaning —
add only one letter — to find out where

she comes from — *mab, mad, mal, mam, man,
map, mar, mat, maw, may:* this mother of all

morphemes, root from which I come.

Tuesday

As she irons
      cat's-eye wrinkles
out of his
      sky blue button-
down cotton shirt,
      cord hanging
from the overhead
      kitchen light,
sprinkler bottle handy,
      mother's eyes—
as father walks through
      the door—seem
to contemplate nothing
      in particular
though she sees every
      thing even rouge
still faint on the collar
      flattened under
the nose of the iron,
      but the blur
of her hand, its swift
      shadow rising
on the wall behind her,
      is all I see
before his head hits
      the floor.

The Rundown

"How done is gone?"
—Rita Dove

1.

Her run-down moccasins
with the backs bent flip-flop
from the bedroom to the bathroom
to the living room where two suitcases
hold her part of the three thousand six
hundred some odd days of their marriage.
Time is running down, and she thinks
about his three black suits, the line
of pin striped, navy and charcoal gray
all weather-worsted wools, tropical
tan and seersucker summer suits,
double and single breasted blazers
with golden fleece buttons. Why
does a man need three black suits?

2.

And all those ties: regimental stripes,
muted somber solids, a few pale polka
dots, nothing whimsical dangling
from the carousel. That first year
she brought in a paisley was the first
time she tasted malice running
down and through the salty sting
of his words. She counts seventeen
pairs of shoes, lined up, toes forward,
facing her, colors running from coal
to kangaroo: wing tip, cap toe, tasseled
loafer, biscuit toe, cordovan, split toe,
even a pair of jodhpur boots, spit-shined
and creased where his foot bends.

3.

Running down the month's worth of white
and sky blue button-down collared shirts
that line his wardrobe shelf, she memorizes
the crisp stiff smell of laundry starch. She
takes a moment to run her hand down
to the drawer in the high boy where his V-
neck cotton undershirts are folded in half,
then to the narrow drawer where all his over-
the-calf socks point in the same direction.
She never learned how to run her fingers
down the seam in his boxers, to fold
them in perfect thirds. Now, the last
ten years of her life running down, she
knows that leaving is not the same as left.

Epithalamion

Everyone knew they'd been nowhere
done nothing but live in the projects.
Too young for much else, they lapsed
into marriage, her hair streaked blonde
with bronze highlights, his bristling
with a Caesar cut. A high school diploma
earned him baker's apprentice while
she quit to play house (without him
climbing in her bedroom window anymore).

She had no sisters or brothers.
He had one of each and a mother
with no husband of her own
which made her hate his choice
and accounted for the bride's
sad face in the wedding pictures,
her amber eyes with the look
of the already caged.

We gave them six months.
They stretched it out for ten
years until his outside children
broke its back, but their crash
proved they'd been somewhere,
done something.

Answers May Vary

All I know is
    before I turned four is
        the day my father
            left my mother because
        he could no longer hold her is
        the day my mother
packed and moved
        us from their place because
            it could no longer hold her is
                the day I left my mother because
            she could no longer hold him is
        the day she left me because
although a daughter I am him
    You see?

Truth

Ash from her cigarette doesn't fall.
Smoke trails up in the air, drawing
her closer to answers the blues have.

She breaks another mirror, tries
to live and hide, knowing it is her,
her beauty that drove him away.

It is easier – so she thinks –
to make up things about him.

Last year, merchant marines   *They do what?*

Nine months ago, with a jazz band   *The band?*

Six months past, on business   *The business?*

This week, working late   *Every night?*

Sleep   *All day?*

And so it goes.
Until she decides
at long last

Dead. Yes, he would be dead.

Then no more lies,
just that last mirror.

Conundrum

Sin, a small word made large
by what?   Circumstance,
decree, the color red, weak-
ness, beauty, her beauty? And
what was her great sin? After
all, it was only that she loved
apples. Not every day. Once
in a while, you know, for the
vitamins needed by the skin.
There she was: haughty, high
toned, innocent as tears, easily
bored and hungry,

a combination slated for disastrous
satisfaction.   Feeding that hunger
made her accomplice to her own
downfall, every time. She thought
Bellevue Hospital a hotel she could
sign in and out of when bills or her
current man threatened to over
take her. That a fall happens does
not explain how or why, just then,
she bites into something delicious.

School Break

Hemmed in by the summer
screen, we peek through sheer
curtains at our mother.

Some days she promises
lovely music, her voice
a tangled blue chant

misting us like sea spray.
The day she doesn't sing
a storm pounds the rocky

place. Sobs drown her
song. Peering in, we see
a pill bottle near her open

hand. Pieces of a broken water
goblet halo her body, splayed

on the parquet floor.
Uncovering our mouths,
we bond beyond her blood.

What
Yellow
2
sounds like

What Yellow Sounds Like

i.

That January day back in '38
somebody picked up a rainbow
and broke the sky in two,
releasing Jamesetta Hawkins
into a two-toned world
that eats up yellow by the dozens,
a yellow so pure it gilds the L.A. sun.

Round faced, blighted by a mole
on the right side of her cheek,
she came prepared to drench
the world in love and agony,
her salty smolder on record labels
not yet named.

By 1953, cat eyed,
eyebrows arched
with the black of a used match,
hair enduringly blonde,
she cut her first record
Roll With Me Henry at fifteen,
making promises
she couldn't possibly keep,
steeping her sound so deep
its punishment feels like protection.

They shorten her name,
invert it like the Bottom.
She becomes Etta James,
too big to be invisible,
canary colored blues woman,
rock gut, gut bucket, bucket
of blood, blood and pluck,

plucked at midnight, nightly
on the 4x4 stage of a juke joint
pulsing with sallow smells
of sweet wine, stale hopes,
smoky dreams bathing
in mustard colored lights.

ii.

They tell her she has to live it
to sing it. They don't tell her
Bessie and Billie had done that already,
so she flings fire for the fatherless girls
who are trying to be women,
razors piercing men with words like
Cling to me Daddy, pleading
with the wrong one
to *Trust In Me,* promising
she'd rather go blind
than lose the man she loves.

And Etta just kept on.

As she opened her veins,
she churned up her roar
to keep other women from dying,
even temporarily, spreading their hips
on bar stools, open toe black
sling back high heel dangling
from the right foot of a crossed leg.

All the while, Etta stomped
barefoot on stage,
platinum hair authentically blending
with the yolk yellow scream
she hurled from the marrow of her voice
scorched and scared,

jaundiced by the freedom
of surviving a rage
simmering somewhere
between heaven and heat.

Life Is Like a Song

Bouncing between break down
and break through, Etta's sound,
a mirror turning lyric inside out
from the first cut. Her songs
the rage of a woman set on surviving,
but she didn't start out like that.

There was once the promise of the sun,
the brush of blonde curls hugging her waist.

Then came the wail
each time her mother left,
the howl for a father
still unidentified. At five,
they told her, *Sing girl, don't back away,*
grab those notes like you own them.

Yellow Privilege

to some is always light brown
or butter, but Etta was not on
the high end of that dream. She
was low yellow. Poor, jute thick
braids with frizzy ends, too dark
to pass, too blonde to pass by,
a sock running down in her left shoe.

How she didn't like being fenced
in, loving the blues. There was no
family name. No grandfather from
Philadelphia. Still, a life arranged
by her talent for triangle songs
and preference for lemon on panther
colored skin, she so full of appetites.

Black and Yellow

Legend has it Minnesota Fats
is her daddy. Yellow remembers
the past. The silence of a legacy
that betrays itself through one
inconvenient drop of blood.

Her momma, a chilly brown beauty
with a brittle smile, loved only jazz
and herself. Her fears and dreams
made Etta crave essential things:
black coffee, platinum hair,
a blacker dress, midnight men,
who wanted her
just for the contrast.

Taste of Yellow

"She jes' gits hold of us dataway"
—Sterling Brown

Though she doesn't need to hold
you down to spoon feed you,
Etta does it every time, the soft
roughness in her voice, churning
solid into custard, in that
place where blues leave
but an utterance, where only
certain sounds reach mystery.

Living there, she is familiar.
She knows where to go in,
how to take your clothes off,
when to give you something.
And with all that, there is still
someone left who is hungry.

Yellow and Blues

Not some color-caste chorine,
Etta nails down defiant mulatto.
Her body a plump fire,
swollen with innocent needs.
She pours herself into a fish tail gown,
arcs her voice with a sound
that drinks up her thirst,
trumpet primed to moan,
bleeding notes through her rant.
Bending some. Blending others,
she guts the places
you can't touch.
Come, meet the blues baby.

At Last

It's the violins that wake me,
not the smell of fried apples,
sunnyside eggs or percolating coffee
hissing as it spills over on the stove,
not the dream of eating left over
fried chicken for breakfast.

It's those violins that open the song
the way the sun opens the day,
removing the darkness from last night.
Saturday. They'd gone to a dance
at the Gayheart Ballroom.
Jessie and her five, yes, five
beautiful daughters,
one of them my mother;
each one told
she is prettier than the others.

First, I watched them,
helped lace them into long line bras,
whale bone cinching their sides,
long leg rubber girdles
pushing years of skin
up and down,
hooking up dark silky stockings
that swished as they walked.

Six strapless *peau de soie* dresses
hung over different doors,
each dress unique
in its dull luster of blue
cerulean   indigo   turquoise
plum   violet   lavender.

Shoes with fabric dyed to match each dress.

Potato salad made. Chicken fried.
Boxes of *Ritz* crackers and mints
in *A&P* shopping bags. Mink stoles
and jackets covering their bare shoulders
as their heels clicked down the stairs.

The blues in those violin strings,
before the flattened throaty yearn
of Etta James, wake me.

Grandmother thinks Etta James too randy
for women from Virginia who do not sweat,
women who fear the funk. Pretty women
who cover their sofas with antimacassars,

but those violins tell me
grandmother is still asleep,
that last night left one of my aunts
or my mother with needs: a strong cup
of black coffee, a piece of slab bacon
and a *Sunday Kind of Love,* at last.

Triptych

•

A man picks me.
He's sure of himself, takes
care of me, he's coherently
common, always on time.

> •
>
> I pick out a man, cook
> what he likes, run
> him a tub of water, iron
> his handkerchief, stare
> into his eyes. He believes
> he's my only lover.

> •
>
> I pick up a man and drop him,
> just like that, in a snap, outside,
> my flock, a gust of motion.

Chile,

Why in the hell you botherin' me now?
Seem to me, you old enough to know a thing or two.

At your age, I thought I knew it all.
Turns out I didn't know shit but that a song
had to have more than words, had to have
attitude. Billie had that. Ain't had but a four
or five note range, but she laid them notes
out for you, girl. Naked. And gave 'em back
with a skirt on. Took me thirty years
to understand where that came from.

Once Dinah was in a club where I was
singin'. I tried to impress her. Sang one of her
songs. Next thing you know, she jumps up.
Turns over the table. Drinks go flyin'. I
flew off the stage, too scared to come back
out. Later she told me *Don't sing nobody's*
shit when they in the house. That's how I
learned what I know. Hard.

So, look-a-here, girl, wear the baddest
reddest lipstick you can find and don't go
lookin' for the sun in the middle of a storm.

Yours forever,
Miss Etta James

P.S.   If you ever hit L.A., look me up.

What
Yellow
3
sounds like

Narrow Crossing

On a burnt September day
I am forced to ferry across
the Narrows from Staten Island
to Canarsie, Brooklyn.

They never ask me if I want to move.
They never tell me I will lose
everything I treasure and will not
treasure anything again as I trade sixth
grade honors for seventh grade horrors:

white anklets for knee socks
cotton t-shirts with petite satin bows
for half-filled training bras and full
nylon slips that leave me cold.

Left behind are white Keds
replaced with Oxford reds
redder than the blood that
now stains my panties.
Sanitary belts fitting sanitary
napkins so thick they chafe me.

This is too much for one day.

Good-bye waves from Sigrid
and Jocelyn leave me broken.
Waves on both sides of the ferry
break, leaving a wide line of foam
and spray and my girlself behind.

Geography of a House

Our first dog, Midge, was tied to the sycamore in our back yard, and she smiled each time she choked herself leaping at diapers and towels on the clothes line. All the magazines on the coffee table had to be in size place order or mother would have one of us for breakfast. Since she worked nights, my older brother and I risked changing her radio station to listen to Jocko Henderson spin Motown, and we played chess until after midnight, and the knight with his L-shaped moves, moved into our house the night our youngest sister stuck her head between the bars of her crib; she screamed, but we took her picture with him anyway. In the morning, our younger brother stood in front of the gas heater with a load of shit in his diaper. Half the picket fence was blown down by the wind. What would keep us kids in? The back door, which was actually the front door, didn't have a lock. The kitchen was at the back of the house, and our cousin's pajama top caught on fire when I tried to straighten her hair, so the firemen broke through my bedroom window to put the fire out. Later while mother napped, our younger sister took money out of the change bowl, rode her tricycle to the corner and bought Chinese food. Cats all over the neighborhood cried. One of our three sisters was so short (we called her Tiny) she disappeared under the dining room table. Each year for the holidays, mother re-papered the dining room walls and hung festive new curtains. We had to dig behind the wallpaper for our younger brother who loved to eat corn starch and paste. Blood spurted from under my fingernails onto clean clothes when rollers on the ringer washing machine ate my hands. I'd have to wash again, so I locked myself in my brother's bedroom to make love to Levi Stubbs, lead singer of The Four Tops. That night, the dining room table read my mind, stood up on its clawed feet and walked out the back door.

Men

"We eat cold eels, and we think deep thoughts."
—Jack Johnson

•

The dust in my uncle's pants pocket
could make his swim-team slim body
soar off the ground,

his father had already flown the coop.
The eldest of his sisters he called Mommy,
his mother, Mother.

Whenever his dreams grew too high to climb over,
he'd summon a strong wind.

Seeing him take off, I grew up pretty damned curious.

•

I was five the first time I had some.

My grandfather held out a teaspoon,
said *Here baby. Taste.*

•

I played with boys, their games, their violent toys,
learned to float *mother fucker* from my mouth
with such grace, I disarmed them.

My mother must have known.

She cried through days and nights
since my father left, pressed
my face into the mirror, yelled
                              You're just like him.

•

Because I had no father, I cultivated part-timers:
one brother, six uncles, one grandfather
                        for one absent father.

•

The girls who become my friends
do so because of my brother. I'm
their ticket. I don't warn them
they'll drown in his waves, whisper
You're so fine into the deep V
of his maroon sweater.

Fever

For near nine
years now he knew
not to need her,

his heart wound
in howl and lack.
Bliss-blind eyes

bear the time
spent. Thrills
came. The cut

clean. His cry
lean. Each sound
crawls with his hunger

for her high
yellow skin.

Light Dinner

for Irving "Papa" Monroe

He'd appear,
pee-stained khakis with cuffs
that break over black spit-shined
cap-toe shoes,

kettle-colored nail-straight hair
sweeping his starched frayed collar,

smudged glasses,
gray-green cast
clouding his eyes.

One day Papa drops
an empty shopping bag in a corner
and himself
in our only wicker chair.

He rocks and stares,
pauses to tear the filter
off a Salem cigarette.

To my warning eyes
he declares
I been smokin' since I learned
to roll corn silk cigarettes
back in Greenwood.

Flicks his ash everywhere.

Papa calls me by my mother's name,
Lillie May, assumes I remember
when the Cleveland Buckeyes
swept the Homestead Grays
for the Negro League championship
back in '45,

or when the Pittsburgh Crawfords
had *Cool Papa* Bell, *Judy* Johnson
and Josh Gibson
back in '35
when colored men and baseball
was something to see.

After hours between rocking,
smoking, flicking, staring,

Papa rocks to his feet,
struggles with his empty bag,
winks and waves me away.
Dinner's light tonight, baby.
Can't find my teeth.

April in Germany

for my father

After the first eight weeks
of basic at Fort Dix,
the second eight at Fort Bliss
and six months of country western
blaring from mounted speakers
in Kaiserslautern, I needed more
than another weekend
                in Vogelweh barracks.

A Friday morning in '56,
I'd heard Mulligan was set to gig
on Ramstein Air Force Base,
and Chet Baker, canned
by Mulligan, banned
in America, banished
to Europe, it was rumored,
would also play, and me without
                a weekend pass.

Ramstein's not Birdland
or The 3 Deuces
with dim lights and clinking ice
in watered down whiskey,
but tonight, GI party night,
stay meant go,
                go see Chet.

Armed with my Rolleiflex
and Leica, using my chow card
as a pass I waved into
the NCO club
packed with GIs
eager as penned in horses
                smelling clover.

Cigarette smoke and rising steam,
swirling bodies clustered between
café style tables
clouded my depth of field
while we waited for Mulligan,
his group and their
                    West Coast smooth.

Before the second piece,
the chant began as question
Where's Chet? By the next,
it thundered into demand
We want Chet. We want Chet
roared through the room
until Mulligan had no choice
but call him
                    to the stage.

Lex Humphries on drums
and Chet, lost in the heaven
that was his horn, jammed
with Mulligan on a make-shift
stage, re-united this one night
in a country not yet walled off
                    within itself.

With my Rolleiflex, I caught Chet
in focus, all else, hazy but worth
the risk of being shot by Polish
base guards, worth the threat
of an AWOL charge, worth this long
cold night of nights before Spring
                    as though it and I had wings.

September 15, 1963

Elvin's mallets, their meaty heads
the color of rotten cotton, assault
taut hollow skin, tense flesh melts
like sweetmeat in the cruel steady
boom of a Birmingham morning.

Tyner's piano keens a torrent of chords
matching the drum's steady blasts,
staccato plunge into the slicing odor
and sting of sulfur cutting through
the luminous Birmingham blue.

Garrison's bass carves a canyon
through the mix of pitched peals, speaks
the grave ache for a quartet of parents
who send their four daughters to church
this sunny Birmingham Sunday.

Coltrane's sax seizes its call as the skin
responds. Keys explode in weary wails.
Roars roll – the rumble tumble of four
dark bodies blown head over head, sounds
spread thick through the Birmingham sky.

My cry, insistent as the quartet's elegy
for Carol Denise almost twelve as I am,
Cynthia, Addie Mae and Carole, already
fourteen. *Alabama,* urgent as the frenzied
aftermath, its music burning Birmingham.

Family Outing

Because she was homesick for the smell
of Virginia tobacco and pit-roasted hog;
because she longed to hear her big brother
scratch out blues on his box; because
she craved the feel of corn silk
and had six stair-step children
before she was twenty-five,
she went to the funerals of strangers.

Twice a week, she'd dress up her five daughters
and the one son, fill a paper bag with saltines
smeared with peanut butter,
the oldest daughter, my mother,
carried, and out they'd go, roaming
the streets in search of a small cluster
of people, darkly dressed, and a hearse
in front of any building.

They grew as professional mourners,
learning funerals the way other children
learn the opera: funerals are opera –
grand affairs, perfumed buxom women,
stalwart-faced men and reserved seating
where they'd sit quietly, hands in laps,
crying on cue to *Precious Lord*
or any deep orchestral chord.

To the Question of
the Handkerchief

Her flesh, flabby and stretched off the bone
flapped like wind-blown sheets on a clothes line
every time she smacked and turned
that pasty mountain of dough
she rolled out on a side board
sprinkled with flour.

A lady always carries a handkerchief; something may spill,
hers tucked in her purse, the breast pocket
on her dress or under the sleeve of a sweater.

Every Sunday, white gloves with pearl buttons
at the wrist, pale blue shantung suit, matching
pill box hat, pumps and handbag, she's on her way
to church, front row, aisle seat. After sixty years
with this church, she earned that seat.

They think I'm white.

For decades, no one knew.
She had wiped up all that blood.

Beauty's Daughter

O, the rub of living with the sun
and being in darkness, through
the fog of rant and rules she hurls
at me since my father left.

She smells frantic,
asks me
Why are you still here?

Aching for the moment
I once pleased her,
learning to read beneath
the lines of mother and daughter,
slicing open the seams

of her abandoned beauty.
I wait until she sets down
dry and wrinkled,
over exposed.

Dining Lessons

Any night in my mother's kitchen, raw
Becomes epicure. Wednesday night was
Italian night, and my brother's high school
Friends would come for dinner. They called

My mother Lillie May *Ronzoni* because she
Home made spaghetti sauce: celery and onions
Sautéed translucent in olive oil, peppers still
Crunchy; vine ripened tomatoes cooked down

And slow, seasoned with a garden of green:
Basil, marjoram, rosemary, oregano and thyme.
The spice of that smell mixed with egg dipped
Veal cutlets breaded to fry in butter. It was

Wednesday, and I knew they would come,
Football appetites, just-finished-practice sweat
Lingering on their showered-in-a-hurry sixteen
Year old bodies. I met my first boyfriend on

Such a night. Me fourteen, teaching him how to eat
Spaghetti with a fork and a tablespoon, how to cut
That veal with a serrated knife right into the grain.

Inheritance

for Kelley Nicole

I walk a mile everyday to visit
my great-grandmother, hoping
this time she won't scream
That bitch is stealing my things
when I walk in the room.

They come, press her back into the bed's groove,
her body curled like the letter C, two-foot long
white hair splayed on the pillow,
her silver bangles, black.

I remind her of the July day she pleaded
with my mother, *Lil, don't beat her,*
of the time she took us in when my parents split.

Get that bitch outta here, she screeches.

I sink into the visitor's chair, watch ice melt
in the clear plastic pitcher on the tray table.

Our last visit, I rub her feet with Vaseline.
She calls me by her sister's name, *Ella Mae,*
speaks to me like I am her, going on about
who would get the china when she dies.

I only want the bracelets.

She props herself up on her elbows,
looks me dead in the eye, asks *Who's left?*

What
Yellow
sounds like

4

The Women in Me

Could cut you with an eye
        sure as look at you.

To church they wear
        Soir de Paris and silk dresses
                they make themselves.

Some wear the slow slur
        of Lester Young
                on their butterscotch faces

because they are loved
        by a parade of men
                in & through their lives.

Some marry, have children,
        some times too many.

Some never marry,
        needing only a space in the bed
                & their thin fingers

drawing on instinct & intellect,
        signifying with a dropped
                handkerchief, a suck

of teeth, a backward
        glance, a raised eyebrow,
                a *Hey sugar* that lies like a purr.

Some drink. Some try to drink.

There was that one time an aunt
        drank herself drunk
                so she could know

what her husband knows
       every weekend
              she locks him out.

Once he threatened to leave.

Without lifting her eyes from the ironing board,
       she said *I'll mourn you for six days.*

Like the rest, she believes no hurt
       should last longer than creation took.

Anodyne

My Great Aunt Fannie carried a knife
in her purse, claiming she could cut any
one's ass too short to shit. I spent many
years scared of her, wondering about
women like her who would roll words
like *sugar* and *shit* thick off their tongues
out the corners of their mouths like sap
running down a readied maple, women
who smoked cigarettes down to the filter
and arched eyebrows with the tips of burnt
matches over eyes that never apologized.

I read about women like her in books,
women with names like *China, Maginot
Line, Ursa,* heard about them in the earthy
grit of Etta James. Women who drank
from colored bottles labeled *Thunderbird, Gypsy*
and *Wild Irish Rose,* a little *Southern Comfort,*
women who fixed men in place with voices
that carved words on top of wounds, said
what they lived long enough to know, that
they would rather die than not live as they had
in places raw with the smell of rut and pluck.

Tangent

Easily, I could savage the ceremonial
black she wears to your funeral.

Erect, in the front row, first seat, as one
by one, people peel off the viewing line

Bend their faces near hers, whisper regrets
into her ear. Knowing you'd go before me

I placed myself here, tenth maybe eleventh
row from the front, on the left side.

The center reserved for your family.
One of the women in nurse's white

Stops at my row, asks *You all right?*
I swallow the blues burning my throat.

Allergies my husband simply says.
Through the afternoon, into the night

I gulp down tear after tear for the nineteen
years you were my lover. You're known,

but no one else knows. All
mourning rights, your wife's.

In Service

for Betty Sanders

What do I dream when I remember
the first time you brushed your moist lips
against mine. I was young, you'd been places,
could please, each time an exploration
larger than yourself, on your way
to rapture in the sunken middle.

What do I dream after putting our last daughter
to sleep, and I crawl under the chenille
bedspread, flannel blanket and pale yellow
top sheet, my body rolls to that middle,
shivering.

What do I dream when in the mirror you're
sitting on the edge of the bed, watching me
slip off my panties, touch myself, my eyes
full of then. And now? Duty dulled,
sucked in a rut row of blues.

No heart stopping cerise, no crease
in my white blouse collar, no flip
of hair caught, no rapid jabber,
no wet skin, no polished rim,
no generous basin to catch the run off in,
no quick run to the store, no petals in pastel
palettes, no centerpiece, no Johnny
Hartman singing *You are too beautiful.*

I want a man, but no one dares
thrust his tongue in my mouth
since you, their shining prince, ambient.
Me, hermetic, in hand-blown glass
when twice a day a surprise of light
breaks through. Your reflection

swirls on the thick wall of one side,
slides smoothly down the other,
every hair on my body alert,
each hand in service.

Middle Passage

As I run
just ahead of a seam
in the sidewalk
being ripped open
by wrung-out hands
a child emerges from my left side
wraps her legs around my waist.

My right hand holds the hand
of another daughter
whose hand holds the hand
of a hand who holds another
and so on for many blocks
their feet flying above the concrete.

Hold on I yell,
but children
have their own will.
They drop hands.
I fall back,
naked now.
My open legs
straddle the spreading divide.

Pointing
at a serpent-thick scar
rising on my stomach
one laughing child
reaches in,
grabs the ovary
she says belongs to her.
Another child
screams *Blood*
as she
and my last eggs
slip into the rift.

After Seeing
Kerry James Marshall's
The Black Mermaid

There is a stream cutting through the center
of the garden.   It darkens and swells, and I

don't remember—can I swim?   I cry
yellow tears that spread on the blue blue

water. Faces of family women dead or gone
appear. Their eyes, splitting open my spleen,

draw yellower tears. One tear ruptures.
A woman rises up through the bluest part

of the blue. She extends her left hand. I
pull back. Her right hand covers the space

over her heart, that breast missing. Roots from
a mangrove drip between the fingers of her left

hand, and in a voice deeper than the black of her
skin she says, *Lose everything.   You will not drown.*

How to Look at This Yellow Girl

i
This yellow girl
amplifies herself
against black.

ii
She travels
atop a black cat
weightless,
a pure vibration.

iii
Who does not favor
this yellow girl, but
love?

iv
Wheat fields sway
in the wind. Yellow
goldens.

v
When yellow was
first flung, amber
eyes slanted, she
grew an afro.

vi
The greatest hoax:
a fixed fate for
yellow skin.

vii
Oh *her*, she's
yellow wasted
skin stretched,
over handled,
the color of baby shit.

viii
The heart of an egg
bleeds yellow
on everything toasted.

ix
When white's too
much to want, high
yellow will do.

x
A history lesson:
tragic black bucks
and yellow girls
with lemon tongues.

xi
Like a black-eyed
Susan, this yellow girl radiates
from her dark center.

xii
The smell of hops,
spill of foam
over a frosted glass
ignite the yellow flame.

xiii
A black boy
makes it to the ivy
league, so he pins this
yellow girl like a letter
to his varsity sweater.

xiv
The future of this yellow
girl: holding her own
among biscuit-colored
friends with dark urges.

xv
Why *not* imagine
this yellow girl
eating up the sun?
She is her own
weather.

Intuition

And somewhere in the wilderness of making
decisions, my great-grandmother said to me
Everything don't need to be told. Some things must.

I knew then but not when I would write
poetry, for the poet stands outside a locked
door and rings the bell once, knowing that

once can mean always, that one more is too
much, that just enough opens the door
of the page onto a mirror where beauty

and ugly show up, unreconciled,
where what it feels like to love and be loved
is seen, that place between don't and must tell.

The Muse Speaks

1.
There is more to you than loops
of letters tying and untying every

word your body speaks
as it meets the earth

carrying time around
with each breath, heavy

and hot, felt as much as heard
your head full of rhythm, your heart,

the stories of others, and me
listening although right now

you notice only your own gesture
your own routine, while I linger

long enough for you to swell
with all the breast and beast

you will spill onto the lined
yellow pad, the tight skin

of your language rescues
me from damp silence.

2.
So hungry,
I fell for the new blues
from your tongue.

You give me
a new name,
coaxing my weathered
body onto the page.

Each time you
tap on the door,
I draw the curtains
and let you in.

You want everything.

You tap again.
I'm alone
behind the door
willing you away,
back to your life,
your wife.

Knowing you want me
makes me despise
and miss you
with love and a question—
how long?

3.
No two o'clock in the morning
plea will rouse me.
Your reputation grows,
but that's not what stirs
me. Not tonight.

You've been inattentive,
no word in weeks.
Ours is not yet a settled
relationship; it needs more

than your mute glance,
your grunt of want.
It's not some one-nighter
notched on your belt.

You're a poet,
you know what to do.

Find another way in,
an unhinged transom,
a sash that gives way.

Remind me what I give,
how I captivate you
in captivity, forgetting
the labor of your making.

4.
These damned cosmopolitans
have me hazy with nostalgia,
margaritas sprawl me
on the divan
with a salty afterglow.
These constant calls,
so beneath you.

You once brought me lines
that slid off the glazed skin
of your parchment.
Now? Slack surges,
filling me with your flat funk,
your boiled-down blues. Wide
words spread so thin.
You've said everything.

Acknowledgments

GRATEFUL ACKNOWLEDGMENT IS MADE TO THE FOLLOWING PUBLICATIONS
IN WHICH THESE POEMS FIRST APPEARED:

African Voices "Hair" (appeared as "About Hair")
"At Last"; "April in Germany"; "September 15, 1963" were featured on
  From the Fishouse audio archive (www.fishousepoems.org)
Brilliant Corners: A Journal of Jazz and Literature "What Yellow Sounds
  Like"; "Black and Yellow"; "Taste of Yellow"; "At Last";
  "A History of Beauty"
Brooklyn Review 20 "Life Is Like a Song"; "Yellow and Blues"; "Yellow
  Privilege" (appeared as "Three for Etta")
Brooklyn Review 21 "Dining Lessons"
Brothers and Others: An Anthology of Black Women Writing About Black Men
  "Light Dinner"
Cave Canem Anthology VII "Conundrum"
Cave Canem Anthology VIII "Dear Miss Etta James,"
Center for Book Arts Broadside Publication "Intuition"
Center for Book Arts Broadside Publication "Part 4" of "The Muse Speaks"
Crab Orchard Review "The Women in Me"
Gathering Ground: a Reader Celebrating Cave Canem's First Decade
  "Family Outing"
Heliotrope "Tuesday"; "After Seeing Kerry James Marshall's
  The Black Mermaid"
Los Angeles Review Part 2 of "The Muse Speaks" as "The Muse
  Counts Down"
Medicinal Purposes "Etymology"
PMS: poemmemoirstory "Beauty's Season"
Rivendell "Family Outing"
Warpland: A Journal of Black Literature and Ideas "Middle Passage"

I WOULD ALSO LIKE TO ACKNOWLEDGE:

my parents – Paul Nathaniel Johnson, Sr. and Lillie May Monroe Johnson

my siblings – Paul "Chuck" Nathaniel Johnson, Jr., Barbara Jean Emanuel,
Michael "Buddy" Johnson, Claire "Sherri" Goll and Paula Smith and their
families

all my aunts, especially Ellen Jean Higgs Gates and Esther Beatrice Stokes

all my uncles, especially Clyde Hall, Bill Higgs, Elwood Stokes and Charles
"Chuck" Ward

all my cousins, especially Biff and "Sweekins"

my grandparents – Irving Walter Monroe, Sr., Jessie St. Clair Royster
Monroe Collado, Irene Morton Johnson and Walter Johnson

my great-grandparents – Primus Monroe, Lillie May Gordon Monroe
Gray, Jacob Royster and Minnie Weathersbee Royster

my forty year friends – Hennie Goeloe Alston, Sheila Brewster, Sharon
Hall, Shelley Lynn Johnson, Phyllis Rogers and Leslie Solder

my thirty year friends – Sabrina McCoy, Cynthia Reyes and Yolanda
Reynolds

my mentor – Charles Evans Inniss

my Cave Canem family, especially Cornelius Eady and Toi Derricotte
whose vision made Cave Canem a reality, all the talented fellows from the
1st ten years and those to come, the amazing, generous faculty, Carolyn
Micklem and, of course, Dante Micheaux

my Medgar Evers College family, especially President Edison O. Jackson
and my brilliant colleagues in the English Department chaired by
Elizabeth Nunez

Frederick Douglass Creative Arts Center, especially Doris Jean Austin
and BJ Ashanti

Faculty at Brooklyn College, particularly Lou Asekoff, Geri DeLuca,
Pat Hopkins and Rick Pearse

Elizabeth Alexander, Epifanio Castillo, Jr., Kwame Dawes, Krista
Franklin, Janice Hassan, A. Van Jordan, Virginia K. Lee, Rodney Terich
Leonard, Richelle McClain, Sapphire and Tracy K. Smith for their love,
friendship, guidance and support

All the blues women, then and now, especially Miss Etta James